SQUEAK the Ball Drawing Pad

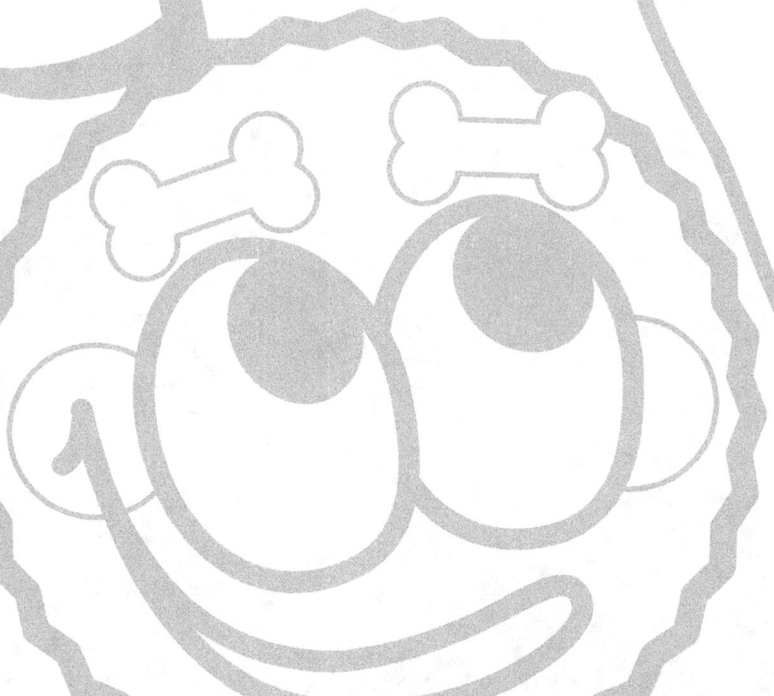

FUN

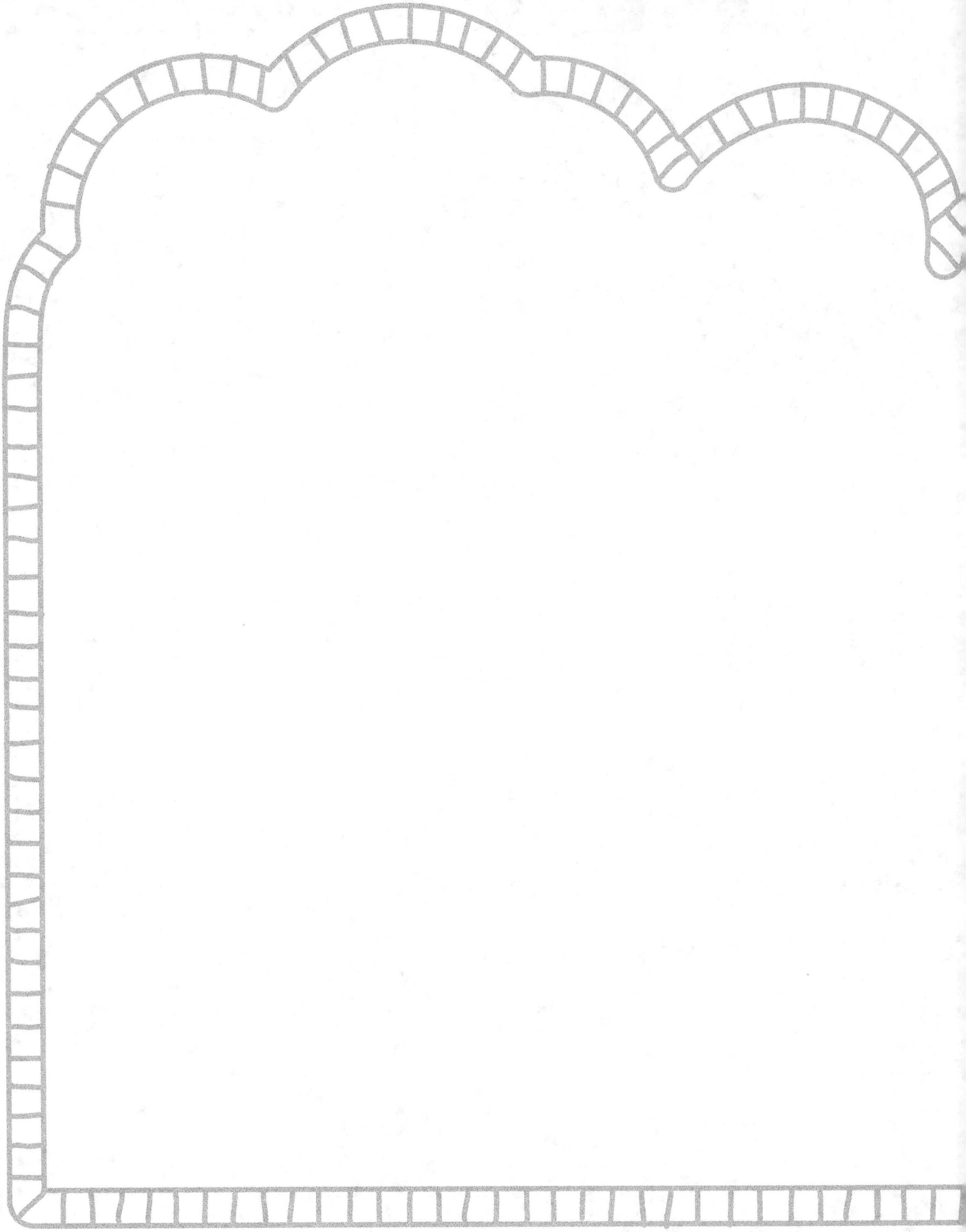

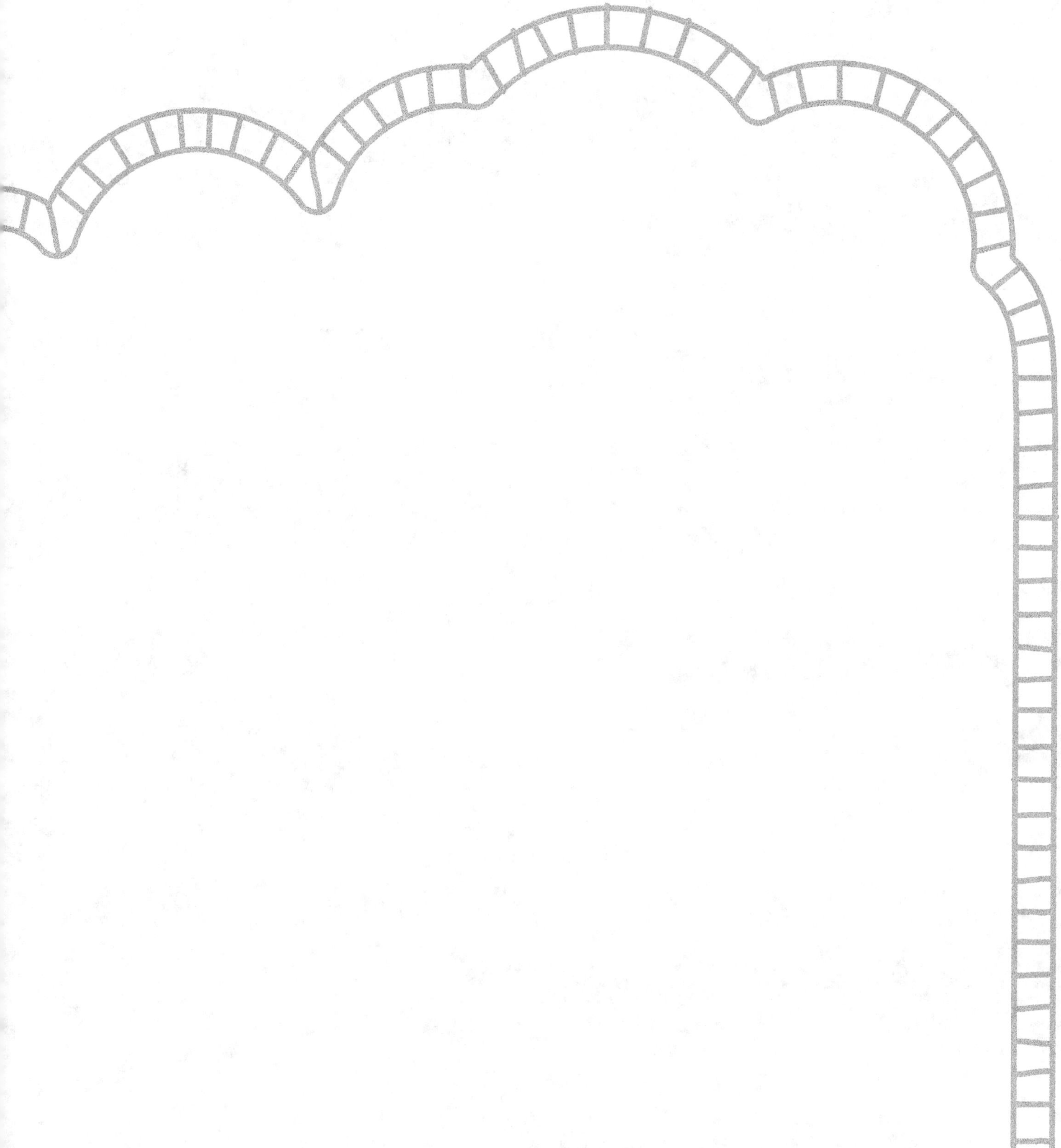

FUN

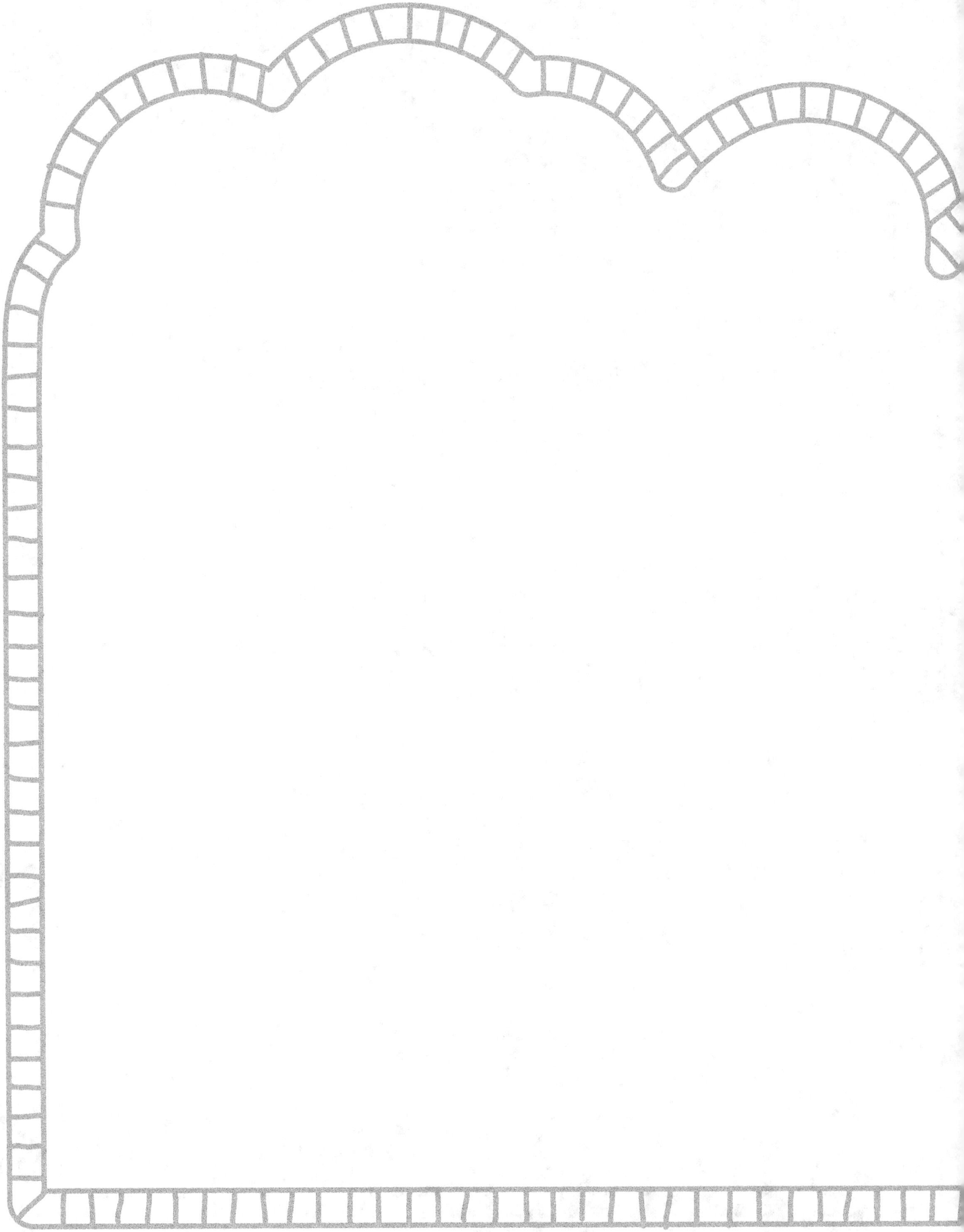

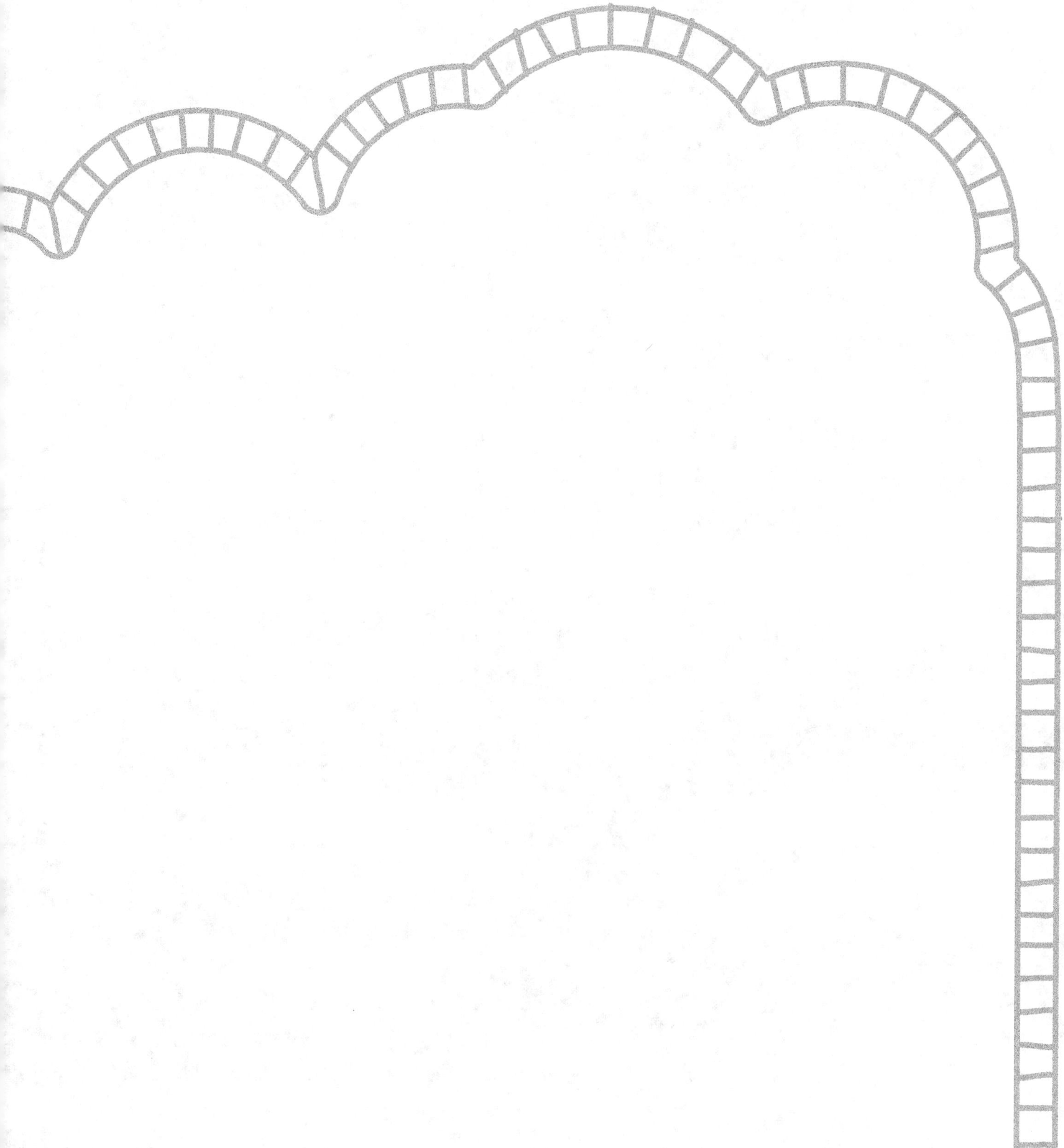

FUN

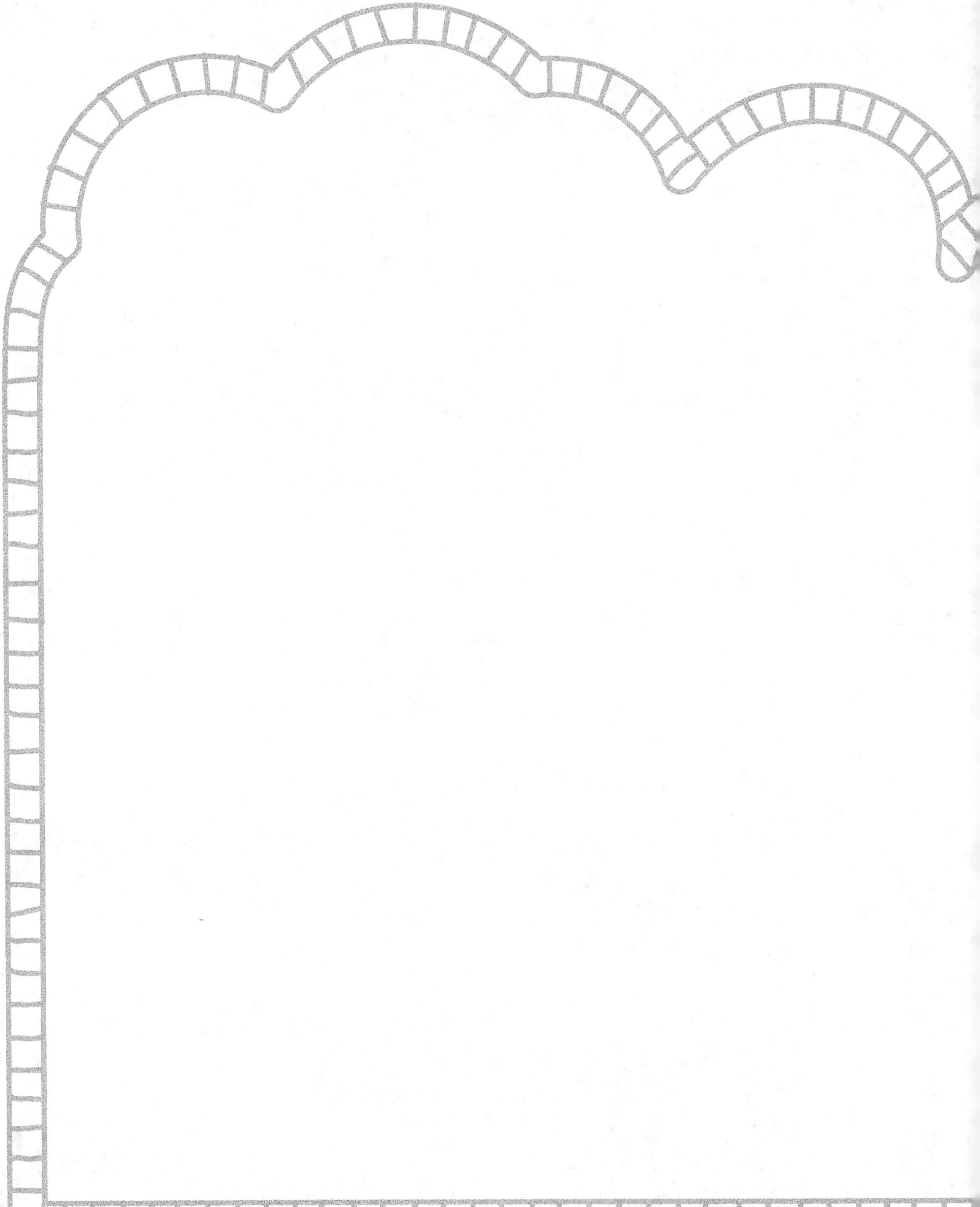

FUN

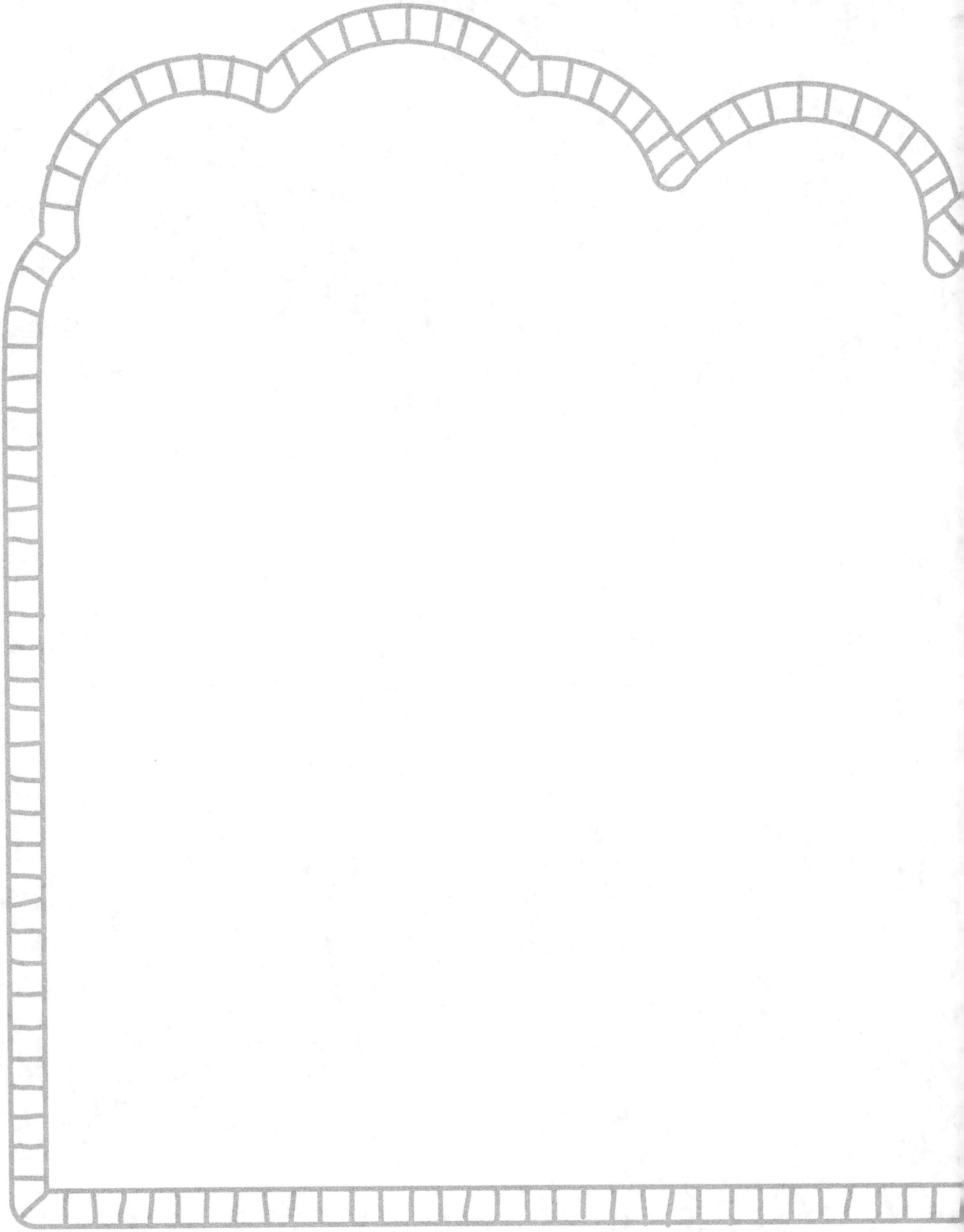

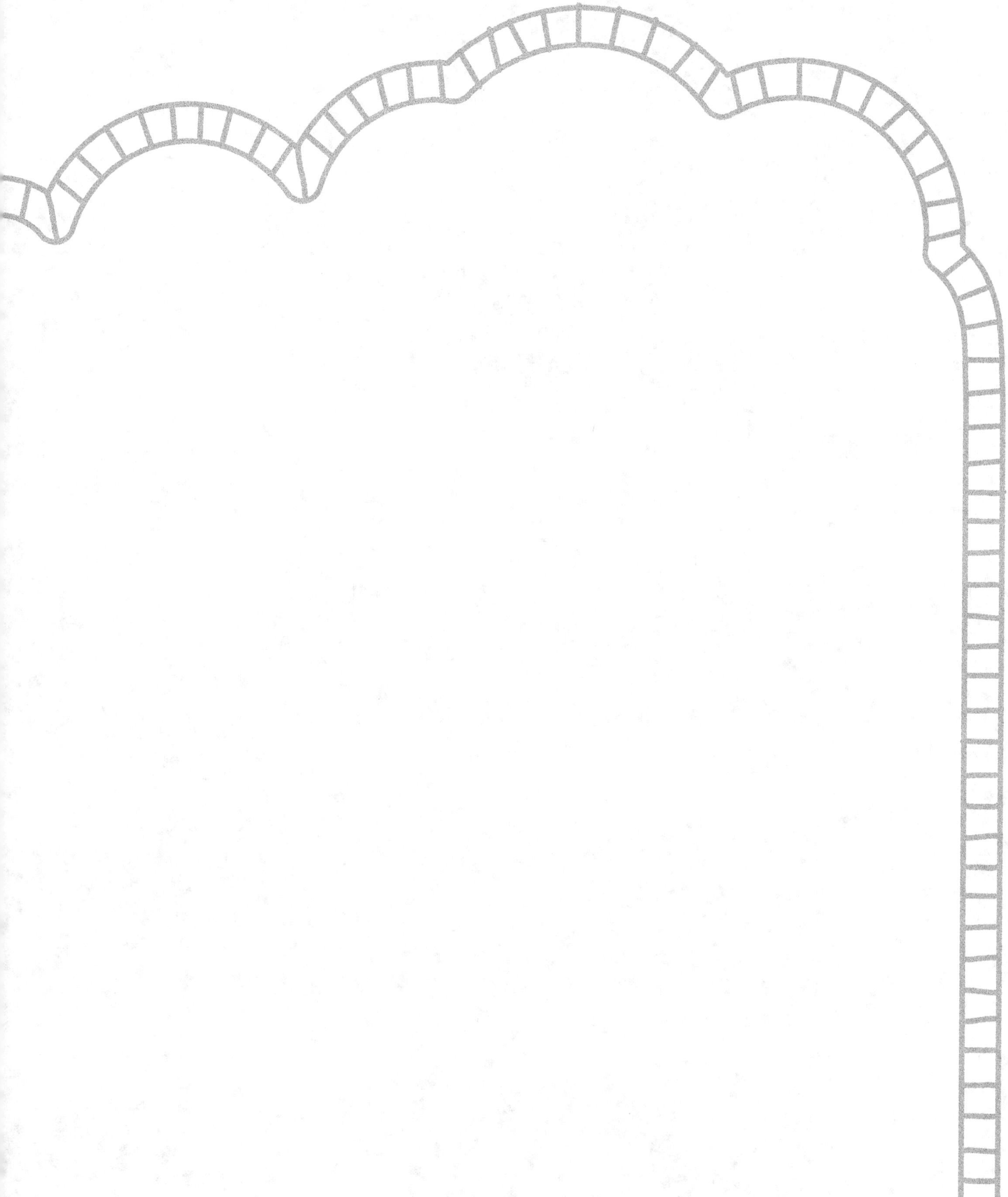

FUN

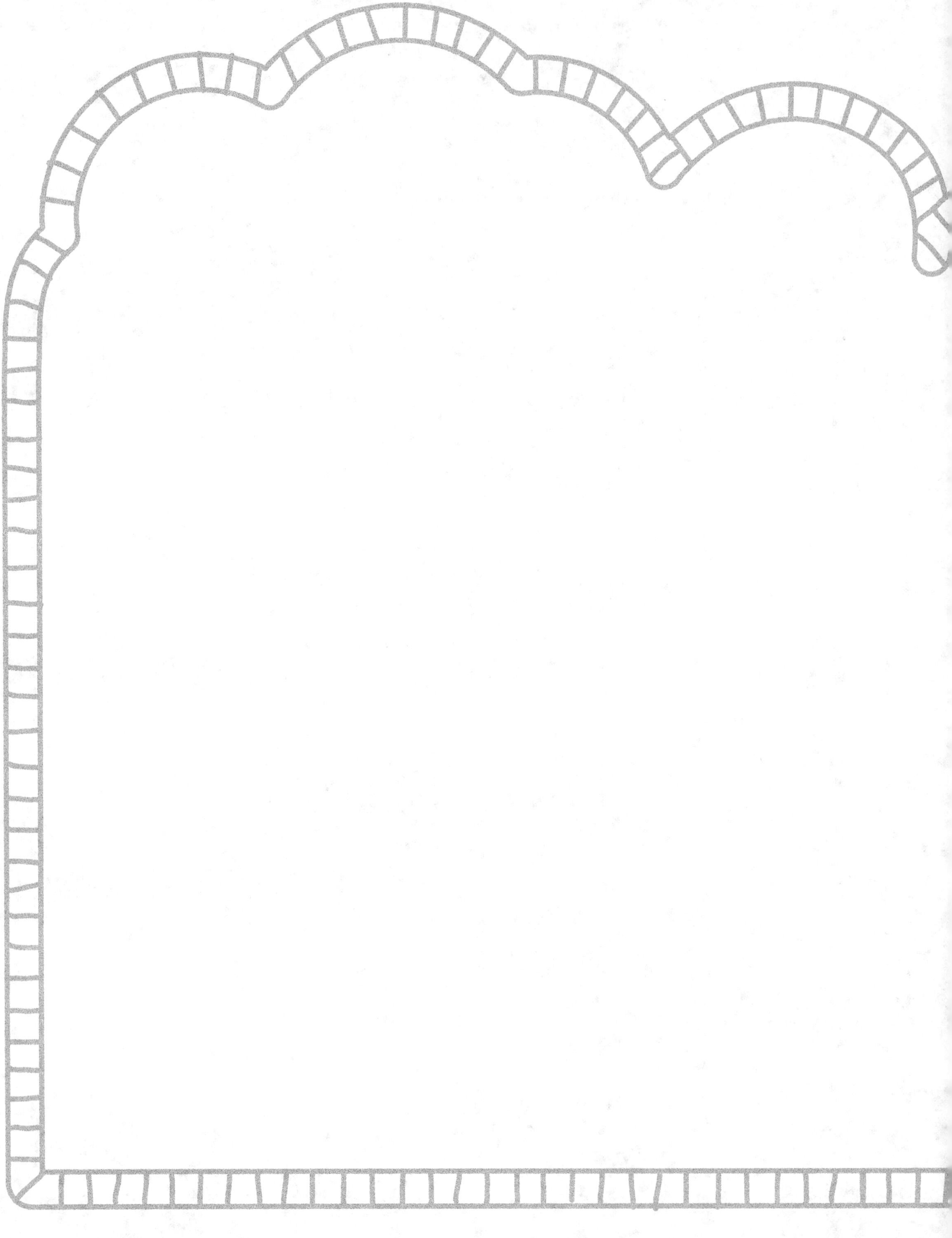

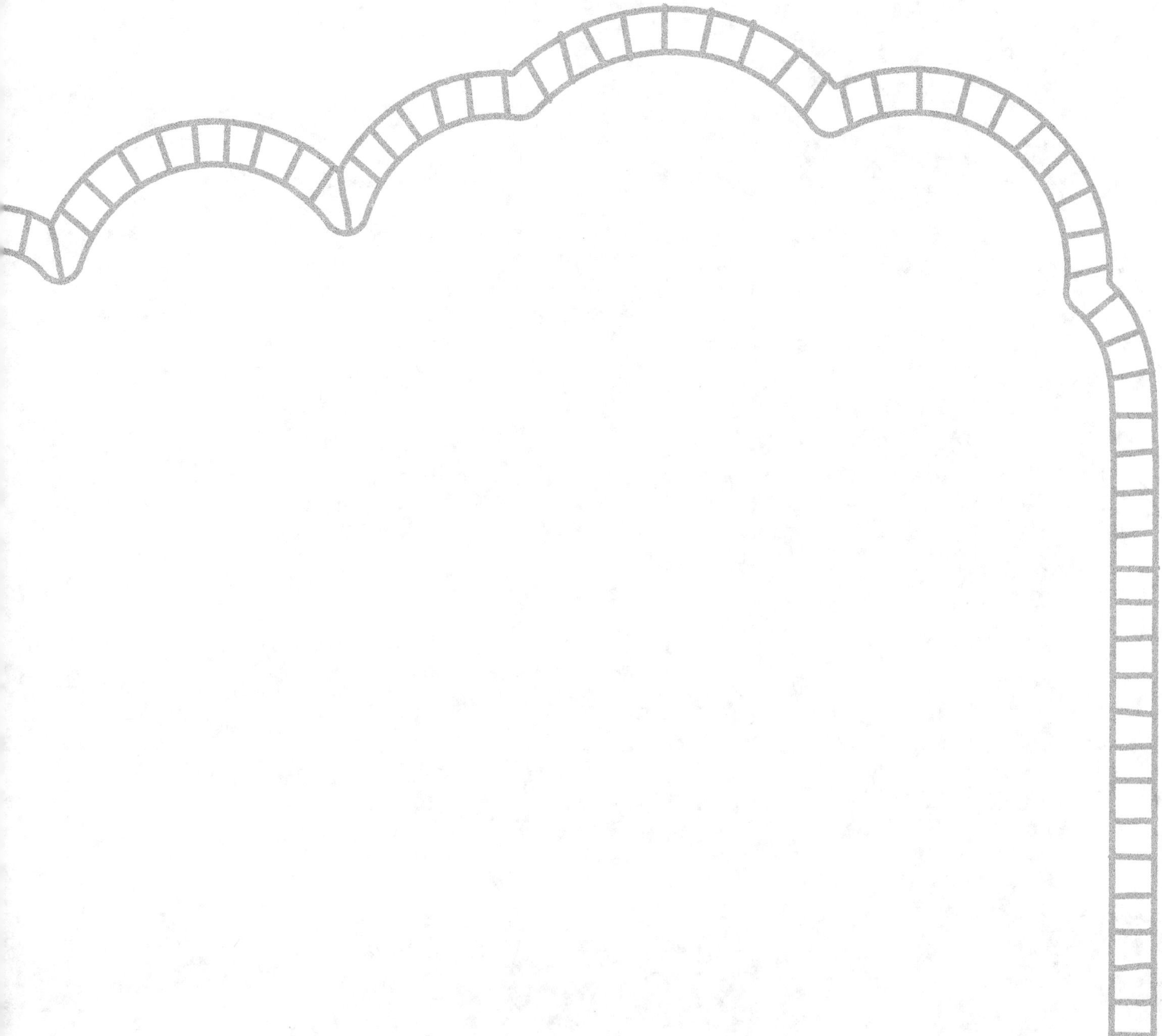

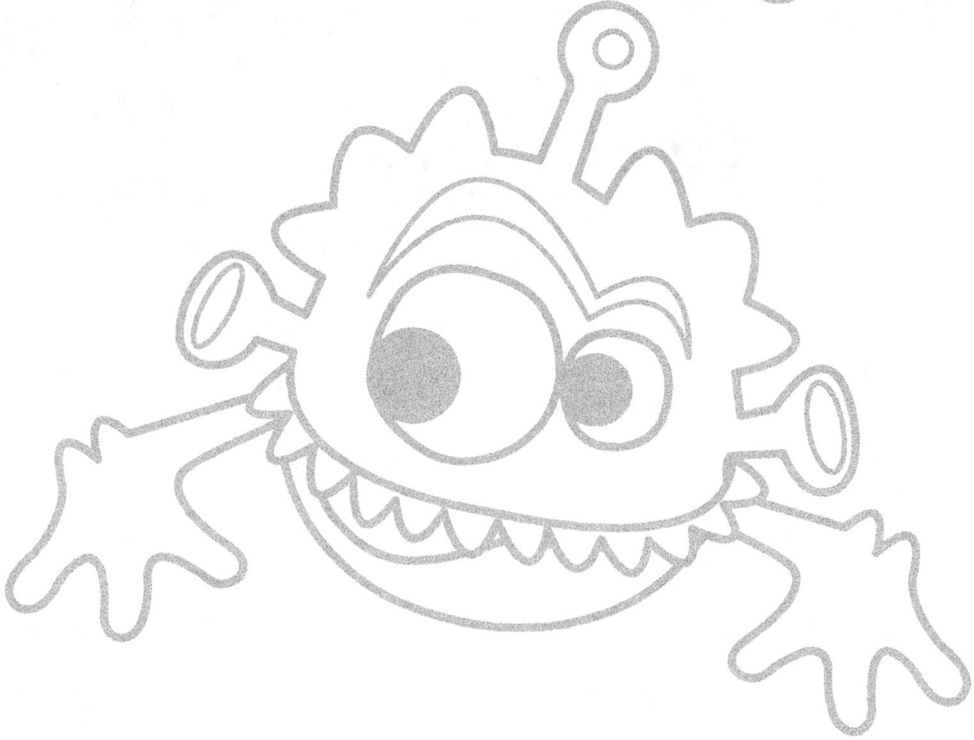

a

CHRISTINE
MACKENZIE

design

www.zookytheterrier.com

www.ingramcontent.com/pod-product-compliance
Lightning Source LLC
Chambersburg PA
CBHW081200180526
45170CB00006B/2163
* 9 7 8 1 5 4 5 3 5 3 7 5 2 *